37INK

SIMON & SCHUSTER

A No-Nonsense Tour for Those in Mourning or the Merely Curious with Denise, Heaven's Receptionist

Welcome to the Afterlife

Taryn Delanie Smith
Illustrations by Maria Krasinski

37INK
SIMON & SCHUSTER
New York Amsterdam/Antwerp London
Toronto Sydney/Melbourne New Delhi

37INK

SIMON & SCHUSTER

An Imprint of Simon & Schuster, LLC
1230 Avenue of the Americas
New York, NY 10020

This book is a work of fiction. Any references to historical events, real people, or real places are used fictitiously. Other names, characters, places, and events are products of the author's imagination, and any resemblance to actual events or places or persons, living or dead, is entirely coincidental.

First 37 INK/Simon & Schuster hardcover edition October 2026

37 INK/SIMON & SCHUSTER and colophon are registered trademarks of Simon & Schuster, LLC

Interior design by Lewelin Polanco

Manufactured in China

1 3 5 7 9 10 8 6 4 2

Library of Congress Control Number has been applied for.

ISBN 978-1-6682-1246-2
ISBN 978-1-6682-1248-6 (ebook)

To my community,
who have taught me so much about
love by sharing with me their grief.
Love endures all things.

Thank you for loving me,
for loving Denise, and, most of all,
for loving each other.

And to Shoshannah's Stanley.
A dad who lives on in love,
and stories told by his daughter.

Welcome to the Afterlife

In death, it's been said by many that a great precipice yawns open before our spirits. White light, peace, and the open arms of those who have preceded us in death beckon just beyond.

Oh, such mysteries that elude the Living! For it is only there, in that welcoming white light, we might have all questions answered, and that great unknown of all the universe shall unfold . . .

. . . Really, this is so dramatic.

If you wanted a tour, you could've just said so.

I don't usually give tours to the Living. But hey, you only live once, right? Ha!

Actually, that's kind of up for debate up here . . .
You know what? Never mind.

I'm Denise, Heaven's receptionist. **Come on in.**

Unless you wanna keep chatting with Geoffrey over there.

He's been giving the same tour since, like, the dawn of time.

I can take it from here.

Most people find their Afterlife pretty lovely.

Heaven really is great,
no matter who you are or what you believe.

If you're looking for someone in particular,
they're probably around here somewhere.

Oh, hey, Abe!

There's loads to do Upstairs.

There's horseback riding, bingo,

pickleball, flying lessons—

that is, if you want the **angel wings**.

Really, I don't bother with them.

They tend to get in the way of things.

You'll find that everyone gets along pretty well Upstairs.

Earthly worries don't matter so much here.

See, Upstairs, you **forgive**. We make it easy for you to not only forgive others, but to forgive yourself as well.

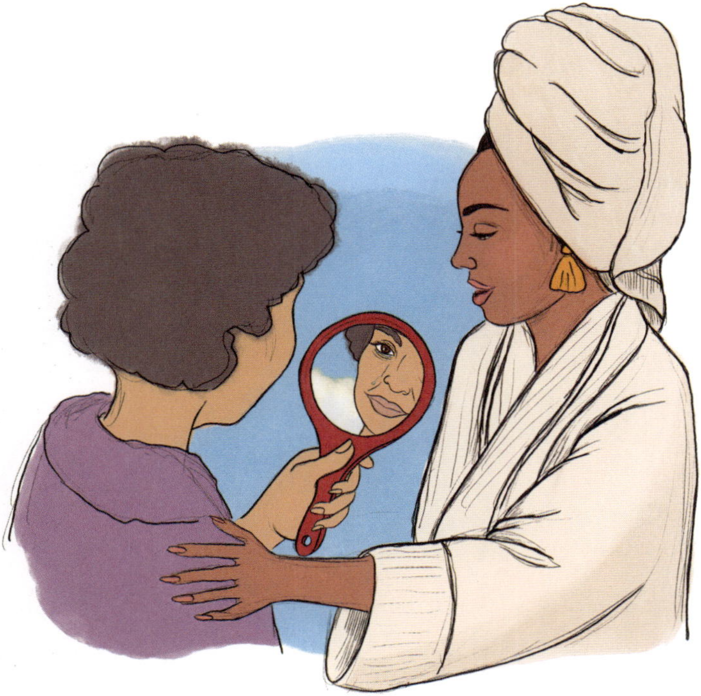

It's a big perspective shift, you know?

Once you're here, you realize that perfection was never the point of your life. If you're lucky, your time on Earth is spent making mistakes, **not working toward perfection**.

If you were perfect, how would you learn the important stuff anyhow?

Kindness, compassion . . .
and, our big favorite, **forgiveness**.

Some spirits end up earthside for some time. They're there for what we call UBD.

That's **Unfinished Business Duty**.

I can't officially condone haunting, but listen, everyone has business, and I tend to mind my own.

That's what I'll say about that.

It's more common though that you earthside folks—**Livings**—tend to have the most unfinished business.

There are always things you wish you'd done, things you wish you'd said before your loved ones transitioned to life up here.

You should know,

those you love who have passed are watching over you with a level of understanding and forgiveness that I don't think the Living can fully comprehend.

Now that's not to say there aren't
consequences for your actions
during your time on Earth.

It's sad to see the cruelty
some are capable of.

I don't understand it. I never have.

But there's no room for cruelty,
malice, or prejudice in Heaven.

And then, of course, there are all the pets.

Some of you rack up a lot of pets in a lifetime. They're all Upstairs waiting for you too.

You can't imagine how many treats we go through a month.

I've always thought the adage "all dogs go to Heaven" is funny because, well, of course they do!

But so do all other beloved animals. They wait patiently for their **Not Yet Passed** (or NYPs, as we call you) to come get them.

I've spent many a lunch break here, you know. **It's peaceful.**

At one point, we sent these creatures to Earth, and the Living have the free will to decide what to do with them . . . and generally they choose to love them.

Love is so ubiquitous a thing that, when these creatures return to Heaven, they wait for the Living to join them, so deep is their love in return.

Gwen never owned a cat in her life, but wasn't she surprised to find all the neighborhood cats that she fed and loved for thirty years waiting for her here?

They never forgot her love, and neither did we.

Are you coming?
You gotta keep up. This place can be a maze, and we don't get a lot of Livings up here.

Ha! So don't get lost. AR (Angel Relations) would have an attack. **Come on!**

There's always a chair being saved for someone here at the pool. One day, you'll find someone you love holding your spot with an extra towel.

(You're not really supposed to do that . . . There's an online portal to reserve another seat, but . . . we usually just look the other way.)

And who do we have here?

Mr. Davis, it's good to see you.

**It's always good to see you, Miss Denise.
And it's always good to be seen.**

I'm doing a tour, so I can't chat long. You have an appointment to visit your family downstairs today, don't you? You better get going. Traffic on the Cloudway will be packed come dinnertime.

Don't I know it! I lost track of time, sitting here with the sun on my face.

I never miss watching family dinner.

Once they get to telling stories and laughing, it feels like I'm right there with 'em.

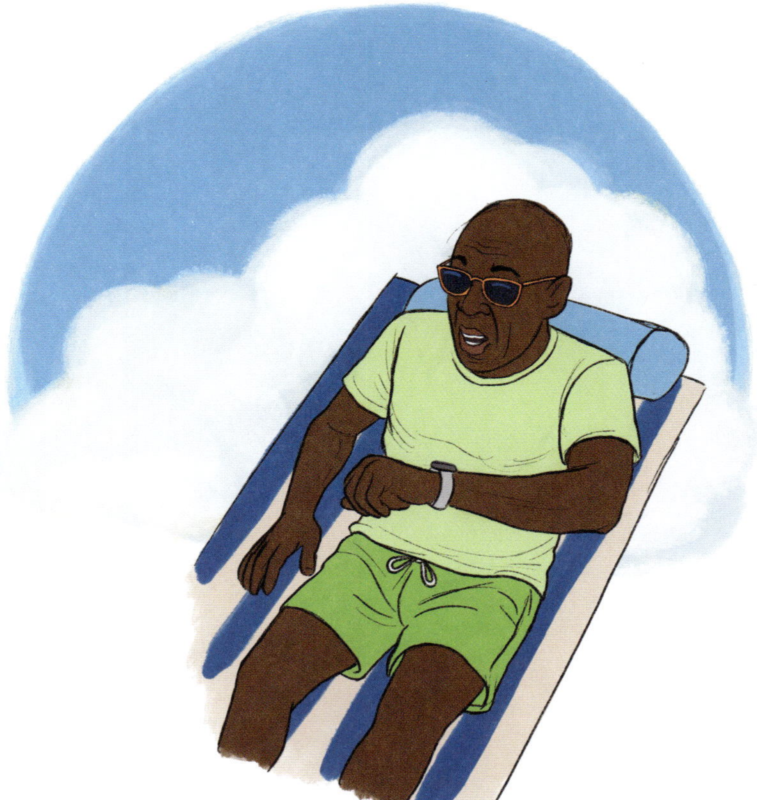

Of course, they don't know I really am.

Bye now, Miss Denise.

Speaking of the time, come along now! Water aerobics starts soon, and this place will be a *zoo*.

We have so much more to see. The meadow is beautiful this time of year.

If you're looking for a little angel, well, they'll be waiting for you in the meadow.

We take very special care of our littlest angels.

They're safe here.

They get to learn, and grow, and climb trees.

If you're not here to hold them, don't worry.
There are so many angels who pitch in.

Your little ones always sleep in someone's arms.

There is usually a line of grandmas, great-grandmas, and great-great-great-grandmas waiting for their turns.

And this is my desk.

I've spent every day here
for five hundred years.

And I tell ya, **I've seen it all**.

Just give me a moment.
I've got to check this guest in.

Hi! How are you?

**So, this . . . is Heaven?
I've passed away?**

Well, yes. And no.

Now, now, Laura.

It's alright. This is Heaven, yes. But you haven't passed away. You've just **passed on**.

You haven't gone away. You're right here with me and your loved ones.

What about my family? I'm a mom.

Yes, yes. I know.

There's no way around the fact that they will miss you terribly, Laura. We can't ease that for them. You love your family, and they love you.

Grief is just love in a different outfit.

It's a crap outfit.

Ha! I like you.

You'll see, there *is* peace for you here, Laura. It will take the ones you've left on Earth longer to find it. It's always harder for the ones that stay behind when we set off on a great adventure, isn't it?

**I suppose . . . I suppose I do feel peaceful.
I just worry for them. They'll be without me.**

Come with me.

Your family and friends who beat you here weren't expecting you so soon, but they're waiting for you.

You mean I'll see them all again?

Of course!

Laura, you'll still see your children who are
Not Yet Passed too. They'll never be without you.

Really?

Yes, really. You can see them anytime you like. You can walk beside them on a sunny day, hear their laughter, sense their frustration on the days things aren't going their way, sit beside them when their grief hits them in great big waves.

They might not always realize
it's you with them, but you'll be there.

And when they tell stories about you, which they will, you'll know it, and you'll be there.

Remember that time you burned the turkey and they had to order pizza? Ha! Good stuff. They'll tell that one every Thanksgiving.

How is that possible? How can I be there when I've passed on?

Love, I suppose.

It sounds more like magic to me.

Love *is* magic, Laura.

It's the closest thing to real magic there is.

Oh!
You're a
hugger!

Thank you.

Anytime.

The beach! I love the beach.

I know. Your people are waiting for you there.

The thing about the Living is
they all think they're so
different from one another.

That there are good Livings
and bad Livings.

But you should see my files!
Everyone has one.

Yes, even you.

Most Living people have done
both good and bad things.

The bad things, well . . . I just
hate to see. It's a shame, you know?

But get to know a NYP—watch them long enough like we do—and you'll see.

Most want to be good. Most want to do good.

The **Not Yet Passed** want to do the right thing. They just need the opportunity to do so.

We always mark that in their file in pink, like this, see?

Pink is all the good stuff.

We never miss the good stuff.

We hope for that.

See, the Living make things *so complicated,* if you ask me . . .

Um, excuse me.

Yes, Tammy?

Hello. May I be in . . . the book?

Uh, sure, Tammy. This is Tammy. She's chosen a very . . . interesting eternal ghost form. We're not sure why she chose to look so scary, but it just goes to show that goodness comes in all forms.

So don't be alarmed! She's just a tad different. Tammy, go ahead and show them around a bit. I have some paperwork calling my name.

Ah. Good. Hello.

My name is Tammy.
I know I am rather . . . ghoulish.

But good hearts, you'll find, come in all shapes and sizes.

I don't remember much of my life.

Too long ago now to remember.

But from what I recall of Earth, it can be very cruel indeed.

However, there is kindness where you look for it.

Do not forget to look.

You'll find sauerkraut, which is so tasty.

And drinks with very small umbrellas.

And Livings who look up at clouds.

And very small rodents. (Not for eating but for petting, Denise says!)

Babies with little feet and tiny shoes.

And there are bubbles.

And there are sunrises and sunsets.

So many very good things about you Livings that I like to watch.

Most of all, I like to see your reunions here in Heaven.

It makes my eyes leak.

. . . Tammy, have you finished those photocopies yet?

I must go to the magic cloning machine.

Goodbye.

Ah, you're still here.

One moment. Let me finish with Danny . . .

. . . And you're sure you want this to be your ghost outfit? Forever?

Alright then. **Have a nice Afterlife.**

Anyway, how has your tour been so far?

Is there anyone you'd like to see?

I promise they're around here somewhere. We aren't expecting you here yet, of course—so it's not time for your **Reunion Day**. That's what we like to call it up here in reception.

One moment. Here's my next guest now.

Hi, Emily.

Welcome to Heaven.
What would you like your ghost outfit to be? Also, I have some general intake paperwork for you to fill out, if you don't mind.

Is my sister here?

Yes, of course she is. Annette's been waiting for you for a while. She helped plan your whole Reunion Day party. The paperwork can wait, for now.

But promise me you'll fill it out by the seventh, okay?

Susan in AR is going to chew me out for another backdated intake form.

But what can I say? **I love Reunion Day.**

Oh! And who is this?

Hello there. How'd you get so far from the heavenly meadow?

Today I'm going to be a butterfly and visit my mama.

She's earthside.
With my brother.

Well, that's very good, Luna. I suppose I shouldn't hold you up then. You're very busy. When you're all done with your visit, come sit with me. I want you to tell me all about it.

Now I really need to be getting back to work.

As I always say, I hope I don't see you soon.
But eventually, I'll be seeing ya. **Ha!**

And please, have a full life. A good life. Tell stories.
Dance if the music is good.

Dance even if the music is bad.

Remember, you have an audience here in Heaven, after all.

To watch you live your life
is your loved ones' favorite pastime.

(We don't get a lot of channels up here.)

Even though your loved ones who have
passed on aren't there beside you,

you are never alone.

RESERVED

To my community,

I will never be able to adequately put into words my gratitude for your enthusiastic, loving support over the years. I hope you will enjoy this gift to you. Beyond that, I hope this book will find itself in the hands of someone who needs to smile after loss, or anyone who loves the idea of an Afterlife that is colorful, joyful, inclusive, and has a pool.

I *do* believe in an Afterlife. I believe in laughter. I believe love doesn't go anywhere. It's far too full, far too transcendent, to yield to time or mortality.

I believe God has a great sense of humor, and I might have just signed myself up for a heavenly nine-to-five when I inevitably make my way Upstairs. I'm cool with it.

So, to all of those who love Denise—and, most especially, to anyone who has loved so profoundly that in their grief they find themselves looking up—this is for you.

Love always,
Taryn (and Denise!)

Acknowledgments

To my incredibly talented illustrator, Maria Krasinski: You have brought this world to life in a way no one else could. Thank you for sharing your gift with me and the world. Thank you for holding whimsy, and color, and joy so close to your heart the way you do—it flows right through your pen.

Thank you to the entire team at Simon & Schuster for your belief not only in Denise but in me! Most especially, Dawn Davis, who I feel honored to learn from as an artist and as someone who would like to leave a legacy of being a woman who fearlessly champions women. Dawn, you are a fantastic example to follow. Thank you for your patience and mentorship. I will continue to look to you for inspiration long after this book goes to print.

To Maria Mendez: You are a literary force and a thoughtful and gentle spirit. Thank you for your hard work and kindness throughout this journey.

To my agent, Kathy, who has gone above and beyond to make this project come to life—I will cherish our friendship. Thank you for taking a chance on me.

To my manager, dear friend, and fellow griever, Shoshannah—you will never know how much I truly appreciate all you do. I endeavor to be worthy of your unshakable belief in me. Thank you. I love you, my girl.

To my entire team: Kiana, Hannah, Ana, and Conor. Thank you for being my rock and guiding me through uncharted waters such as these.

To my lawyer through this complex process, Matthew Dysart—you a real one.

To my family, my brothers, and especially my darling husband: I love you. Thank you for keeping my feet on the ground.

And to my grandma Pat: I wish you could hold this book in your hands and see your name written here, so you would know just how deeply I will always love you. I checked with my publisher, and they will get you a copy Upstairs. I know you are by the pool—enjoy!